# LEARN WHAT ACTING CAN DO FOR YOU!

DISCOVER how the skills taught to actors can *rejuvenate your social life and jump-start your professional career!!!*

LEARN THE SECRETS ONLY ACTORS KNOW! Re-invent yourself! Improve your speech and shape the sound of your voice. Learn to relax, overcome shyness, banish bad nerves, negativity and achieve calm. Learn to address an audience, or conduct a successful one-on-one. Over decades, countless students, in a range of trades and professions, have profited from the lessons taught in the author's ACTING FOR NON-ACTORS classes in NYC, now summarized in this short, comprehensive, handbook.

Part textbook, part romantic parable – It's not about becoming an actor (though reading it won't hurt dedicated thespians) it's about *learning from acting techniques* IN ORDER TO BETTER PRESENT YOURSELF AND PROSPER IN TODAY'S WORLD - *no matter your age or origin.*

**AN EXTENSIVE APPENDIX IS PROVIDED FOR IMPROVED ARTICULATION AND SPEAKING OF THE ENGLISH LANGUAGE.**

# ACTING FOR NON-ACTORS

*a handbook about*
*Employing Acting Skills to Succeed*
*in Business and Social Life*

*and to*

*Better Speak the English Language*

by Sidney Eden

ACTING FOR NON-ACTORS
by Sidney Eden

Library of Congress # TXu-1-907-016
ISBN: 9780-0-9968086-06

Book design: Doug Barron
Published in the United States of America, 2015

ActingForNon-Actors.com
Acting4NonActors@gmail.com
facebook.com/Actingfornon-actors-452969694875149

SidEden@verizon.net
sideden.com

*To*
*My Loyal Son,*
*Scott*

# TABLE OF CONTENTS

# FOREWARD

This book summarizes a course I created and taught to hundreds of New Yorkers beginning in the early 1980's, when I was asked by one of Manhattan's leading "learning centers" to teach an acting class. Because there were already enough actors, or would-be actors, working as waiters, I directed my class toward amateurs and called it ACTING FOR NON-ACTORS.

My students ranged from high school age to eighty years old and came from a variety of trades and professions: doctors, lawyers, office- workers, mayoral aides, television producers, executives, phone-sex operators and cops, you name it. I enjoyed it, but retired from it after a few years. Since then, other acting teachers, here in New York and elsewhere, have appropriated my name but not my ideas. A title, or name, cannot be copyrighted, but what they teach has little to do with this book. Skip those classes, read this book. You'll save money and learn more.

# PREFACE

*Prefaces are like speeches
before the curtain.*
- W.A. NEILSON

She was the most beautiful thing I'd ever seen. But I was too old for her and we both knew it. Still, I wanted to help her.

Then, out of nowhere, she said, "Ronald Reagan changed America."

When she introduced herself, along with the other students, at the beginning of my class, I guessed she was from the Coast. Most people from California speak well and without accent and the speech of this young lady – let's call her Ms. Nibs – was well-articulated and free of regional influence.

Now we were alone and the class was over. She had asked to speak with me privately and, evidently, she sincerely wanted my help.

"It was his acting skills which propelled him to power, " she insisted. Now, I was even more certain she was from La-La Land; not because of what she said, but the way she said it. I was pretty sure Ms. Nibs was from the Golden State; Orange County, no doubt; Nixon Country.

My sense was strong we came from different backgrounds and, at first, I suspected her of being an opportunist, a well-manicured female on–the-make. But she had beautiful legs and a smile like Audrey Hepburn.

"Why not say he changed the World'?" I ventured, playing Devil's Advocate.

"He changed America AND the World," Nibs said, correcting herself, "and I feel his acting skills played the greatest part in his success."

I've seen Elizabeth Taylor, up close, at her best, but this girl could give Liz competition in any beauty pageant. I wasn't in the mood for political arguments, but that Devil in me made me say,

"True, he changed things, but for better or worse is the question."

"That's NOT the question, it's not the point at all," Nibs snapped. "Forget the politics of it. I'm saying his acting skills are what made him powerful, so powerful he changed the country. He was 'The Great Communicator,'" she said, pettishly.

I said, "Acting can make you powerful and he was a student of the Art, or craft, or whichever you call it. He was proud of being an actor. His parents were liberal people, rather 'Bohemian,' according to son, Ron, and big supporters of FDR. He came from modest means and had altruistic values; studied diction, lost his Midwestern twang, became a radio announcer. Had an eye on Hollywood so, when he went there and signed with a studio, he studied acting, I'm sure, quite seriously." I was happy to be in agreement with her for the time being.

"I'm saying he was an incredibly charming man," she stated.

"So is President Obama. How else would he have achieved such a high position? All politicians try to be charming. The similarities between actors and politicians grow greater every day. I think everyone who runs for the office of dogcatcher and above should be forced to study acting."

"I agree," said Ms. Nibs diplomatically, but she couldn't control her enthusiasm for the man. "Though no one succeeded like Reagan," she threw in.

"In being charming? Franklin Delano Roosevelt was pretty damn charming," I said, firmly.

"Can you teach it?"

"Teach charm?" I said. I had to stop and think. "To be charming onstage is one of the most difficult things in the world for those who aren't already charming. Girls used to go to 'charm school,' learn how to walk with a book on their head, talk properly, that sort of thing. Maybe, they still do; have 'charm schools,' I mean. Today, for those who can afford it, they have Image Consultants who charge hundreds of dollars per hour. They mostly use video cameras."

"Can you teach it?" insisted Ms. Nibs.

"To be charming? If you're not already charming I can teach the things which might make you so," I told her, quite honestly.

"Such as?" said Nibs.

"To smile."

"To smile?"

"To learn to smile," I repeated once more. "To smile when you don't feel like it and convince people of your honesty is an important asset. A good actor knows that. That's basic Stanislavsky. Take a happy thought. Learn true concentration. Then, there's the quality of one's speech, the projection of thought and feeling, how to relax, in short, how to present yourself and, how to prepare yourself, all these things may be learned from acting because only acting teaches all of these skills."

I could have gone on and said that ninety-six percent of American schools no longer conduct acting classes, yet, according to authorities, interviewers and pollsters, the qualities business leaders value most are speaking and listening (reacting), which are the essentials of acting. But I didn't say any of this to Ms. Nibs. She was a smart girl (whether or not I agreed with her politics) and I could sense she was already in agreement with me about the profitability of learning about acting. Nevertheless, I said,

"Frankly, I'm surprised a well-bred young lady such as you are doesn't know all these things already."

"Maybe I do, but I just need a refresher course," Ms. Nibs said flintily.

"What do you know about Stanislavsky?" I asked.

"I've heard of him," Nibs said, uncertainly.

I liked people in my classes to know about the Art of Acting as developed and taught by Constantin Stanislavsky (1863-1938), co-founder of the Moscow Art Theatre. Famous American acting teachers such as Lee Strasberg, Sanford Meisner, Stella Adler, Uta Hagen, Herbert Berghof, Robert "Bobby" Lewis and Maria Ouspenskya (the fortune telling Cassandra of Lon Chaney, Jr.'s WOLFMAN) all taught their own versions of Stanislavsky's "Method." Some journeyed to Russia to meet the Master, some did not (Ouspenskya acted in his company), but all based their teaching careers on their version of his precepts.

Modern acting books are largely concerned with Stanislavskian principles and I meant to convey them to Ms. Nibs, as I do in this book.

Actors have an edge on other people. Nibs sensed that. Those who study acting, or even participate in acting classes on an elementary level, profit over those who do not. Simply reading about acting can be profitable.

In my classes I ask that all participants select a text – a piece of poetry or a monologue from a play. Using that text I try to impart the best way to present the words (which must be memorized) and, through those words and the emotions contained in the words, I teach the student about acting.

Nibs insisted on working privately. I said "Okay," and I told her to familiarize herself with the precepts of Stanislavsky and the teachers who followed after. I said we would discuss the topics covered in these next five chapters:

FOCUS, PREPARATION, PRESENTATION, RELAXATION and ARTICULATION, i.e., the proper pronunciation of the English language.

Nib said it all sounded fine to her and we set a time and place to meet the following week.

* * * *

In this compact package you will find techniques and exercises employed by performers. They can be helpful in your career or, even, in your retirement. They can be of value to you in how you present yourself to, and the manner in which you are perceived by, others. I wish a book such as this had been available to me when I was young.

- Sidney Eden, New York City, 2015

# 1
# FOCUS

## Concentration is the secret...
### - RALPH WALDO EMERSON

I met Ms. Nibs on a bench in Gramercy Park, near the statue of Edwin Booth, across the street from the Players, the club founded by the famous actor whose brother shot Abraham Lincoln.

It was chilly for May. She wore an expensive-looking tennis sweater and shivered from time to time. I tried to forget how beautiful she was and spoke to her as would a Dutch uncle.

"Focus - concentration – is the most important factor in life," I told her. "It is THE essential factor in achieving success in any field, from public service to frying hamburgers. The people we most admire, statesmen, athletes, political exiles, those who have endured in battle, they're all people who have succeeded through perseverance . That 's the kind of focus we seek. Concentration is the actor's mainstay and constant concern."

She made a serious face and nodded to indicate her interest. I continued.

"Concentration and consciousness are bound together. Consciousness means awareness. Ask holy men; that s their definition. Observation of the passing crowd shows that we are surrounded by sleepwalkers. Only the observant are truly alive, aware, truly mindful.

Actors are taught to live in the moment; to

participate; when inactive, to observe, listen, react, and, when necessary, improvise.

Through observation of people, and of the sights, smells, facts and circumstances of every situation, the actor analyzes and remembers in order to portray real people and re-create real events. Actors don't fall asleep on the bus, or bump into people on the sidewalk; they remain alert – always.

The actor becomes the character through means of concentration - FOCUS - as espoused by the Freudian-inspired Stanislavsky. The Actor immerses himself, or herself, in the character in order to **become** the character. The main principle and first step in the process is sense memory (sometimes called affective memory).

It begins with the logic of essential sensory objects, i.e., the things inherent to the environment of the play and its action; things which are part of an event but which are not emphasized by the author and must be created by the actor.

When asked to perform an action or emotion within the context of a performance, the actor employs sense memory by conjuring up remembrance of a similar experience in one's own life; how it felt and looked at the time; the weather, architecture, visual imagery, whatever surrounds the required emotion or event.

Many students say the reason for their enrollment in my class is they're unable, in everyday life, to summon anger. I thought it strange at first. Then, I kept on hearing it. To get angry think of WHY, think of the cause, think of something maddening and outrageous, which happened to you; or think of the Holocaust; or of Trans-Atlantic slavery. Employ your imagination.

Focus. CONCENTRATE.

When required to cry on cue, the actor triggers the process by remembering and re-experiencing the death of a pet or relative. Sense memory requires you, the actor, to recall events that happened to you, personally, not the character. Relying on artificially triggered emotive skills and **pretending** to experience the emotion – 'playing the result' – ends in insincerity; the audience isn't fooled.

When one's sensibilities are fully developed through practice (rehearsal), one can cry as quickly as it takes to hum a few bars of music, or picture a relative's deathbed. Audiences can't wait for the actor to go through mental gyrations, so, the actor finds a shortcut. I know one who plays the main theme of 'Rhapsody in Blue' in his head and tears pour forth in cascades. Proper focus is also employed in the process of NOT crying. Think about it. Focus on Bravery, concentrate on the theme of Courage, **become** Joan of Arc," I said to Nibs. Then, I said,

"Uta Hagen's book, 'Acting Is Believing,' is one of the best on the subject, yet one of the greatest actors of all time, Laurence Olivier, famously said, 'Acting is lying,' which infuriates the Stanislavskyites and understandably so. Olivier worked from the outside in, not from the inside out, as we are taught to do in America, but there is truth in his statement. When, for instance, we die onstage we are employing the imagination alone; we have no previous point of reference.

I am not advocating getting through life by lying, in this highly-competitive, dog-eat-dog society, but, so-called, 'appropriate' presentation of unpleasant facts, 'spinning,' and other forms of mild prevarication, may be forgivable under certain circumstances. In our modern society, the ability to sugar coat the truth seems, almost, a necessity.

On film the actor 'acts' for only seconds at a time. The camera holds but two minutes of film. The actor waits all day long in the trailer, or elsewhere on the set, trying to stay in character, trying to remain FOCUSED.

So, the actor develops a technique to bring the character back into being when the lights and camera are ready, some trick of mind, some evocation within the 'mind's eye' which triggers the character back into being on cue. You, too, must learn to do this," I told her.

"An audience is manipulated and led by the actor or the actor ends up with egg on the face. The actors are onstage, for the most part, because they want to be loved and, instead, they end up being hated! They've lost. Audiences don't return to see plays they don't like.

But, through the focused efforts of concentrated individuals intent on re-creating, as if for the first time, something they have rehearsed, over and over again for days or weeks, the actor directs all learned vocal, physical and mental technique to the task of controlling and satisfying, an audience. Sometimes the seats are filled, sometimes not, but the show must meet the same high standard in either case.

In performance the actor focuses mind and body on a particular goal, or consecutive set of goals, occurring over time, during the span of the play, or film, and brings the goals to fruition one at a time. The process is almost the same for a speech or presentation. A positive attitude, a form of 'thinking makes it so,' must be the mind-set. The key to success in playing a specific role is not to successfully PRETEND, but to make yourself

BELIEVE that you are the character. It's the same in real life.

The successful working actor is one who is able to apply this same belief system, this trick of the mind, toward the goal of achieving status with casting directors, agents and stage directors who might offer employment or, in some cases, stardom.

Acting is highly competitive. Usually, employment comes after many previous rejections. The strong become more determined, while the weak fall by the wayside.

Being 'discovered' is a myth, except for certain movie folks who materialize while being extras. Once 'discovered,' they're taught to be real on camera for 15 seconds per take, through trial and error. Few stars are made overnight; most have acted for years on and off-Broadway, in student films and independent movies, until, finally, casting directors, agents and others 'discover' their true worth, and cast them in a sitcom (or some such) where they become famous.

Doggedness is the determining factor in success. This kind of devotion has meaning beyond the Method and should be significant to non-actors. Aside from talent, concentrated devotion is the main ingredient in succeeding in the Theatre." I paused, significantly. "And it's the same with everything else."

She nodded her beautiful head in enthusiastic agreement.

I was getting to her, but I was, also, beginning to feel a little like an insurance salesman, out on this bench in Gramercy Park. Still, I went on.

"You focus when you drive a car, or hammer a nail, or you suffer the consequences. Double tasking is an

obstacle to success. Concentration means refusing to
succumb to discouragement.

In the Theatre, when they don't want what you have
you have to get better at what they want.

Does that make sense?" Nibs laughed and I
resumed.

"When he actor errs in performance the actor
strives to recover through concentration. Similarly,
non-actors, in everyday life, correct their errors through
concentration, though they probably don't think of it as
I do. Make a mistake, you try on second opportunity to
correct it. Without proper focus the result is negligible.
Developing a subtext, as an actor does, helps. A mantra
spoken to oneself, as simple as 'I MUST SUCCEED,'
will suffice it. The actor has a text, why not you?

The Theatre is a microcosm of Life. The actor
maintains FOCUS on and offstage. The craft requires
the dedication of a religious fanatic, a commitment
to perpetual awareness of, and receptivity to, stimuli.
This devotion (often generated by the search for Fame)
produces a power of focus so strong it simulates that
of auto-suggestion, so strong that it may be employed
telepathically. Think of 'cold calls,' that is, calling
someone without an introduction."

She looked off wistfully, then, brought herself to
attention.

"There must be exercises for this," said Nibs.

"For focus and concentration? Definitely, but don't
let anyone catch you practicing them in private"

"How so?"

I said, "In acting classes teachers will ask you to
perform certain everyday actions aimed at expanding
your imagination and your emotional responses. They

may sound silly, but give them a try." I enumerated them
for her and list some of them here for you. Practice these
exercises for FOCUS and CONCENTRATION via
expansion of your imagination.
1. Prepare and drink a Breakfast drink and find it
   rank.
2. Shave, or do make-up while seeing oneself in
   mirror.
3. Portray the effect of the stimuli of sunshine.
4. React to a sharp smell.
5. Portray seeing something (you supply the "something").
6. Do the same while hearing something.
7. Portray showering.

*  *  *  *

I found out a lot about Nibs that first day on the
bench in Gramercy Park and she learned more about
me.
"You're one of those Lefties, I know."
I told Nibs none of us could control the
circumstances of our arrival on Earth and that I was
born in Cook County, in Chicago, Illinois, the very
bosom of the Democratic Party. I told her my family
supported FDR and always stood against lynching
and for Civil Rights for African-Americans. I further
volunteered that I had been a Red Baby, meaning, as a
child  I attended rallies for Henry Wallace's campaign
for President on the Progressive Party ticket, rallies
at which Paul Robeson and Woody Guthrie sang, and
African-American leaders like W.E.B. Du Bois and A.
Phillip Randolph spoke.
Nibs told me she was adopted by a wealthy family,

at an early age, and that she had worked on her pronunciation of words and the placement of her voice for years. It showed.

"I've always read aloud and sometimes recorded myself reading poems and stuff. "

I asked her her reason for attending my class.

"I feel insecure sometimes," Nibs said, "and I want people to like me, respect me, not just have men chase me."

The gated private park in which we sat was barred to the public and entrance restricted to residents of the homes which bordered its four sides. One of these was Edwin Booth's four-story dwelling, redesigned by the famous architect, Stanford White.

Booth owned his own huge theatre on nearby Sixth Avenue. It stretched from 22nd to 23rd Street. This brother of assassin John Wilkes Booth was the highest-paid actor of all time, receiving $50, 000 in gold per performance.

In 1888, in his home across from the Park, in seclusion and humiliated by his brother's foul deed, Booth happily surrendered his large home in fraternal benevolence, and with Mark Twain, William Tecumsah Sherman and a handful of famous actors of the day, founded a club. It grew in membership until it included many famous men and women through the decades, until the present time. Cagney, Bogart, Sinatra, the Barrymores, have all been members. It is a place where actors might meet and mingle with eminent practitioners of other arts and professions.

This bench in the Park across from the Club was not the place to be conducting a class, but she was a nice girl and I planned to escort her on a tour of the facility when we completed our lesson-talk.

"You asked me to select a piece. Not something that requires deep emotion, but to say it with honesty."

"Directly; simply but well-articulated."

She said she had chosen Portia's "Quality of Mercy" speech from Shakespeare's MERCHANT OF VENICE.

"The quality of Mercy is not strained;
It droppeth like the gentle rain from heaven
Upon the place beneath. It is twice blest;
It blesseth him that gives and him that takes.
'Tis mighty in the mightiest; it becomes
The throned monarch better than his crown.
His scepter shows the force of temporal power,
The attribute to awe and majesty,
Wherein doth sit the dread and fear of kings;
But mercy is above the scept'erd sway;
It is entrhroned in the heart of kings;
It is an attribute to God himself,
And earthly power doth then show likest God's
When Mercy seasons justice.

She stopped there, though the speech was longer. It is written in iambic pentameter, ten syllables to the line (so that "throned" is two syllables). You might think the "supposeth" stuff unnecessary, but it's good, sometimes, to put your tongue between your teeth and speak properly. She spoke with unaffected conviction and I tried not to fall more deeply in love with her.

I am aware the Reader may think reading Shakespeare, or reading anything, to be unnecessary, but if you are to profit from the techniques of acting – or prosper at all – you must deal with words. You had better cross your "t's" and articulate by dropping your

jaw on "sway" and "crown" and "monarch." You may
use this speech, or any other by Shakespeare or by
any other author, but find some material with which to
monitor and improve your speech.

Work on it. Memorize it. It requires – you guessed
it – concentration. I suggest you continue working on the
piece you select for the remainder of your life.

When Nibs and I returned to the Players, as a reward
for her good work in speaking the words of the Bard, I
told her something I knew she would like to hear.

It was related to me by one of the Clubs past
Presidents, Roland Winters, a well-known Hollywood
character actor and the last to appear as Charlie Chan. I
appeared in a couple of productions with Roland, a man
much older than I, and we became friends.

Throughout his life and career, Roland had been a
colorblind Democrat who stood for racial justice. He
was a superb raconteur and toastmaster and he was pals
with, and appeared with, many great stars including,
James Cagney.

Roland, when under contract to Warner Bros.,
worked with Ronald Reagan, too. He told me,

"I never worked with a nicer person."

I did not mean this as an endorsement of our
fortieth President but said it, merely, to please Nibs. Yet,
Roland said it with a gravity which convinced me of his
sincerity.

The information put Nibs in a swell mood and, after
a tour of the Club, we made a date to meet the next
week in the same place at the same time.

# 2

# PREPARATION

*Always prepared. (Semper Paratus.)*
- LATIN SAYING

We sat on the same bench one week later and I said, "The actor's career develops in public but the actor develops in private. Preparation, hand in hand with concentration, leads to proper presentation. That's the goal whether you're an actor, a statesman, or both." I smiled when I said it because I was thinking of President Regan and Nibs knew it.

She was lovely in jeans, a denim shirt and a Yankees cap.

"The preparation must be there in either case. Things don't just happen. In order to succeed you must be *ready* to succeed. You must be prepared. 'I am a firm believer in luck and believe that the harder I work the more of it I'll find.'"

"Who said that?" she asked.

"I did," I fibbed. "No, Stephen Leacock," I confessed, "a Canadian humorist," and I proceeded.

"Men don't go onstage without checking their fly, and ladies don't make entrances with their hair all in a tangle, unless it's called for in the script."

In this celebrity-worshipping society we constantly see actors being interviewed on the boring subject of how they 'researched' and prepared for their performances. Imagine some jerk asking Edward G. Robinson how he prepared for LITTLE CAESAR! It's commonplace and, maybe, enjoyable for people to hear such puff pieces because preparing for a role IS serious business. The degree of preparation the actor undergoes bears application, and should be a guiding light, to the life of the non-actor.

Actors research a role like mad. Remember, they're attempting to immerse themselves in the character through concentration. They're focusing on the character through printed and visual materials, which are available to them in libraries and museums and, now, even on the Internet. Each role demands a new set of facts and one ends up learning a little about a lot of things. Preparing oneself through these inspirational materials is a transformative exercise of the imagination.

Just as each new role is a challenge, so, too, each new obligation in life requires study and analysis before presentation. The event may be an interview. The challenge may be the initial board meeting as CEO, or a speech, or presentation demanding one's very best effort. Preparation is crucial. The first rule of the Theatre is 'Never Assume.'

When you drive a car you cannot assume no one will step out from behind a blind spot."

" You slow down," said Nibs.

"You use your imagination and say to yourself, 'It is possible someone may emerge from that blind spot, so, I will, now, slow down.' Never rely on Habit.

Usually, we live with our being either relaxed or reduced to a minimum. Most of our faculties lie dormant because they rely on Habit. Not so with the actor. The actor's work is to recreate real things as if they're happening for the first time. When acting in a long-running show, the re-creation of events takes place nightly.

Just as the politician makes the same campaign speech time after time and hopes to make it sound spontaneous and heartfelt, so, too, must the actor in a long-running show repeat actions and words night after night as if they're brand new. In any case, achievement of a given goal comes from preparation. Seeming 'natural' (if you're not 'natural' to begin with) comes with practice, rehearsal, preparation.

Habit is incompatible with a successful and happy modern life. Doing the same things over and over is limiting. Rehearsal (the French call it **répétition**) is another matter.

Some people are so-called natural born talents and become immediately successful as actors or actor-impersonator-comedians. Others work hard to come up with the same result. Some even require diction coaches, but they achieve the same effect as the 'natural born talent' through practice. Through dedication one may achieve most anything.

Acting, as opposed to Habit, nurtures. You grow as the character grows. But to be effective you must know your material.

Actors know how to handle hecklers through learned, or improvised repartee. That's preparation. The actor twists the audience around his, or her, finger. Some speakers energize and please a crowd. That comes, usually, from practice; trial and error. Both actor and non-actor alike require proper preparation via repetition.

The actor acts with mind and body. The body is an instrument of expression. To be supple and resilient it

requires proper maintenance through diet, sleep and
exercise. All necessary preventive care and testing must
be accessed, especially, for the eyes. Ralph Richardson
said, 'We act with the eyes.' Watch him, you'll see.

The only justification for gaining excess weight
and increasing the chances of dying is the desire to
become a Character Actor. I mean no disrespect to
them, fellow union-members all of either sex." I was
being a little silly, and trying to get a laugh. She was
hardly a candidate for obesity, but she smiled wanly and
I proceeded.

"The mind and the soul grow through reading and
exploration of the Arts and Sciences, and from studying
Mankind, in general. This is the actor's regime. It's all
preparation, a preparation that never stops.

Anyone who's ever gone to school and studied for
tests knows that, in order to succeed, one can never
study enough. Just as the student burns the midnight
oil in order to learn the answers to potential questions,
actors study their script, over and over, before making
an entrance, even though they already know the lines by
heart. They want to get it right and not miss a line.

Everyone should have a text, a script, words to work
with which explain who you are, and what you want,
and what you can do for the person, or persons whom
you're addressing.

Preparation, also, includes preparing for things
going wrong, and knowing how to deal with them.
It means possessing improvisatory skills; reacting to
the prop that isn't there, or the unreceptive audience.
What is your plan? Have you planned? Why not? Start
planning now for things to go wrong, or how to make

them right in the first place. Learn how to compose yourself in order to deal with potential obstacles."

(In today's climate I remind the Reader that anything you do may be recorded for posterity. If you speak at a memorial or a funeral or just about anything else, in all likelihood, it will be recorded on camera, or on a cell phone, or I-Pad, or other device.)

"Actors learn to deal with the door that doesn't open. Check your props. Test the door. Check the chamber in the gun. Check your fly, again, just to make sure. Ask yourself for the twentieth time 'What's my first line?' The toastmaster, or for the candidate for dogcatcher, must ask him or herself, 'Now, once more, what was the punch-line to that joke?,' before getting up to speak.

As an example of preparedness I give you the great comedienne, Martha Raye, winner of Screen Actors Guild coveted Lifetime Achievement Award. Though she was a featured comic singer-actress from the mid-1930's on, she told me, when I appeared with her in EVERYBODY LOVES OPAL, in a production in suburban Chicago:

'I learned everything I know from Charlie Chaplin,' with whom she appeared in MONSIEUR VERDOUX. This did not make sense because she had been a big star before Chaplin's film, which was released in 1947. But that's what she said.

In the play in which I supported her, I was to appear in a climactic scene and threaten to kill her with a gun. In rehearsals she warned me, 'You better not forget and come on without the gun.'

'That's impossible!' I replied.

But sure enough, I forgot, and she made a fool of me, improvising an hilarious routine, humorously

humiliating me before an audience which howled with
delight at the situation.

'So you came on without the gun, didn't you, Brad?'
(the name of my character in the play) she shouted out to
the audience, which saw something was clearly awry.

'You see, Ladies and Gentlemen, Brad is supposed
to come on, now, with a gun and threaten me and,
then, steal all my money,' she continued, as audience
members bent in half with laughter. I, myself, was in
stitches. Her 'ad-libs,' prepared for just such a situation,
were carefully honed, prepared to achieve the loudest
laughs attainable, even better than the real script. It was
embarrassing, but it was my fault. I was not prepared to
fulfill my given responsibility.

Similarly, the non-actor must address the
requirements of a given situation. If you're to speak
at a n event make sure there's a light on the podium.
Observe where the microphone is placed. If you have
time beforehand, check the P.A.s system. Make lists
of what could go wrong. Don't let things happen and,
then, stand there with egg on your face. ANTICIPATE!
Don't ASSUME and/or rely on others!

Preparation to the actor, also, means showing the
banana before slipping on it; the set-up. Without the set-
up there is no pay-off. Preparation implies anticipation.
In working on a role the actor is taught to discover the
logic of the play: the logic of the character(s); the logic
of previous circumstances, situations and of particular
events. The non-actor going into a serious situation
might profit from these rules; review and observe them.
Ask, 'What would I have to do in order to do what the
character does in the situation? What would I do if I

were the character in this situation?' The character may
be your adversary.
Remember an action is composed of three elements:
1.) What you do; 2. Why you do it; 3.) How you do it."
"What about memorization? That's very much a part
of preparation, as far as I'm concerned." Nibs said.
"Squares think memorization is the hardest part
of acting. Memorization comes to an actor more
easily than to others because the actor is required to
concentrate throughout rehearsal and performance. The
lines become organic through repetition.

I know of no shortcut other than the standard
'trick' of associating a word or section, of that which
is to be memorized, with some other word, or thing.
That's not much of a trick. Memorization is a matter of
concentration and discipline. The more you memorize,
the better you become at it. It's never too late to begin.

Those who went to public schools where
memorization was not part of the curriculum may have
more difficulty than those who have had to memorize,
say, the Gettysburg Address, the capitols of the States of
the Union, or a speech from Shakespeare. But it is never
too late to correct this flaw and I have seen many a
lawyer, or just plain ordinary citizen, rise to the occasion
and please a gathering with something they spent their
time memorizing. Everyone knows the task has taken
discipline, a quality universally admired."

When pressed, people are capable of memorizing
anything. Once, I walked onto a movie set believing that
a page full of dialogue I was to speak was a voice-over,
and that it would be recorded, by me, later, in the studio.
The director shocked me when he said he wanted me to
perform the dialogue on the spot, along with the dozen

actors who were in the scene with me, and with the cameras rolling.

He was a charismatic leader and a powerful actor, and he placed his hands on my shoulders and willed me to learn the lines then and there, and I did so, within three-four minutes, and shot it in one take. I am not smart, but I have disciplined myself to memorize quickly, through practice, i.e., through preparation.

If I were required to recite particular information – numbers and facts – I would feel myself a fool if I consulted a piece of paper. It would show ignorance of the subject. It is far better to know what you are going to say and to say it without reference to a piece of paper. On the other hand if you MUST read a speech or presentation do not rush through it. Establish and maintain eye contact with your audience.

I told Nibs: "Read more. Memorize. Watch television, the news, talk shows, and observe those who speak well and those who don't. Among them will be some newscasters, reporters, politicians and actors who are adept and speak without apparent nervousness. Particularly, watch C-Span, which is free of commercials. Some people who appear there as guests are prepared; others are lacking. Network anchors and reporters are high caliber spokespersons and many are worthy of emulation by non-actors.

On television, ordinary people, executives, first-time guests, and others with less facility, interject needless 'uhms,' 'sortofs,' 'kindofs,' 'you knows' and other unattractive nervous sounds and unexpected stammers. Non-professionals are guilty of the unnecessary repetition of words and phrases largely due to ignorance of how to control nervousness, how to concentrate and relax, something actors deal with lifelong.

Observe people who read from a piece of paper while the hand that holds it shakes from nerves. Again, it is a good rule never to read from a piece of paper when you can deliver the information without it. The actor assimilates the words of his role in order to live and breathe them onstage."

In classes, I told Nibs, teachers use improvisational exercises, involving everyday actions, which, also, might be helpful, to the Reader. Giving specific circumstances and a properly stated intention, these "exercises" are as simple as one wants to make them.

Her are some: opening a door, stroking an animal, hunting for a lost ring , drinking tea, unwrapping a package. Then add layers, complications: you prepare a meal; no one comes. You eat the meal many ways – drunk, bored, hungry, impatient, all carefully defined characteristics with inherent obstacles.

Try one-word improvisations, which draw on and extend the imagination, one-word improvisations such as "America." These exercises lead toward a great awareness and, you guessed it, a heightened state of preparedness.

I realize there are other methods and regimes employed by actors and acting teachers directed toward a better state of preparedness. Gymnastics are helpful. Simple exercises, such as using a door frame for balance, and performing forward leg-swings from the hip, loosens the hip joints.

Singing in the shower – any kind of vocalizing is recommended. Manipulation of the jaw, tongue and lips is a definite aid before public speaking, a means of relaxing, as well as preparing to launch one's vocal apparatus. I will mention this again in a following chapter.

The Alexander Technique aims to eliminate poor physical habits and achieve better body alignment. I am not knowledgeable or practiced in the technique but I have seen those devoted to it practice strange warm-ups just before the curtain's rise, usually stretched out on the stage floor. Check it out. Check out Mindfulness, too.

I acted with a young student of the Polish teacher-director, Grotowski; kid would bang his head against the wall a dozen times just before the play began. I know actors of both sexes who lock themselves in bathrooms at "half-hour" and engage in frightening primal screams taught to them by psychiatrists.

All of these may be helpful, but so is skipping rope. Again, Life is the actor's subject but language is his essential means of expression and therein lies commonalty with the non-actor.

The Alexander Technique is also utilized to alleviate breathing problems and hoarseness, but I have a trick I learned from an expensive vocal coach. I told Nibs about it, as we sat in the park, and it comes under the heading of Preparedness.

Because it will slip otherwise, with a tissue or handkerchief, grasp your tongue with your inferior hand and with the index finger of your other hand massage your tongue vigorously. You will see that the phlegm rises in your throat, your throat becomes clear, and your voice drops, very pleasantly, a notch or two.

Maybe others are lucky enough to have learned this trick, but, since it was imparted to me, decades ago, I

have employed it successfully and often and recommend
it to the Reader.

# 3

# PRESENTATION

*"Be all things to all people."*
- BALTHAZAR GRACIAN

This does **not** mean lying to people.

On the occasion of our third lesson, I took Nibs to lunch in the Great Hall of the Players. We sat beneath the oil portrait of James Cagney, dressed as "Bull" Halsey, the World War II admiral, and we completed our talk in the rehearsal area in the narrow backstage.

There were half a dozen well-known actors there, but Nibs stole the show. The waiters hovered around our table in order to cater to her every need. They got a big kick when I told them she was my niece. One chuckled under his breath, another snorted rudely, and Nibs stifled an incipient laugh. It was June and she wore a summer dress that exposed her slender legs and ample bosom.

As we ate I reminded her of Cagney's famous summation of the Art of Acting; "'Plant your feet, look the other fellow in the eye, and say your words as if you mean them."

This was a while back when people still practiced eye contact and cell phones and I-pads were a Dick Tracy dream. Nowadays, the young enter an elevator and immediately refer to their cell phones to avoid human contact and the syndrome will only grow. If an actor does not make eye contact with another actor, the actor who is not being looked in the eye goes to the director

and complains. Years ago, young people were taught to
look each other, and their elders, in the eye lest they be
considered deceitful. Politicians and other miscreants,
it's true, have mastered the technique of looking directly
in the camera and fibbing, but developing rapport with
an audience of one or one hundred is, nevertheless,
dependent on engagement.

In this context, looking down is a negative. Actors
(most, that is) are taught never to look down at the stage.
To do so inclines the audience to do the same. If you
desire to show your downcast state it's okay, but even
in a one-on-one, it should be used only to engender
empathy. And to look down at a speech perched on a
podium doesn't cut it either.

The trouble with most people is they don't know
how to present themselves and they don't invest the
time to improve. Cagney was right: no round shoulders
and stand up straight. The spinal column moves in all
directions. It's screwed in place down to the lowest
vertebrae. When that screw is out of place one loses
plasticity of movement. A strong backbone is essential.

I told Nibs, "The biggest mistake amateurs make
is speaking too fast. Standup comics, when their gags
fall flat, slow down; they don't go faster. Don't speak
too slowly either. Know that nervousness prompts you
to run through your words. Don't 'milk' the words,
but go slowly enough to be able to measure the effect
your words are having on your audience. But I don't
worry about you. In your case, time and experience will
provide the confidence you need"

"Then, tell me what you tell others."

I say, 'The manner in which you preset yourself
should not be limited by your background. You should

be willing to develop yourself. To do that you must have an ideal. If you want to conform I'm not the one to be consulted.'" We smiled and she continued eating and listening.

I said, "I'm not advising people to act freakishly. I do encourage them not to be afraid to be different. The world is becoming more vulgar by the day. Put something good into everything you do and strive for self-improvement in the way you present yourself to the world; the way you dress, speak and show respect for others."

When I said this I did not realize what "normal" would be years later, meaning today. To be "different" today, when barbarity reigns and anything goes, makes those who dress well, speak well and observe the rules of etiquette stand out even more from the crowd. The sad part is that people are afraid.

I do not see why every question must be answered beginning with the word "so," why words of approval are limited to "awesome,'" "incredible" and "amazing." I feel the phrase "I feel like" should be altogether banned; "I feel" is sufficient. In my opinion, constant use of the word "basically" should be forestalled, and repetitive employment of "whoa" an "wow'" abolished by an Act of Congress.

People who pepper their talk with a constant "you know" show they DON'T know and are probably insecure concerning the subject of which they speak. People who interject "okay?" "right?" and "'guess what?" in every other sentence affront and bore me. And when you are tempted to say "Uhmmm... " before each utterance, pinch yourself , instead. While you are at it, find other means of approbation than the phrases

"totally, totally," "very, very, very,'" "elegant, elegant,"
and the odious "I was like, wow!"

I confess to not knowing the difference between
"really, really" and "really, really, really." And a thing
may be "really" but cannot logically be "kind of
really." Recently, on television, I heard a hockey great,
assessing the talent of Jackie Robinson as "Kind of
really memorable." Know, also, that "nothing" is not a
substitute for "anything" and visa-versa.

When it is your time to speak, do not begin with
"My thing is..." It sounds obscene. Do not surrender
to the flow and say "Like I said," rather than, properly
saying: "As I said...." Naturally, it is permissible to use
slang in order to become familiar with those who know
only slang, but do not allow it to become habitual.

When we discussed the subject back then, sitting
under Jimmy Cagney's portrait, I told Nibs: "Leaders
seek people who are articulate and who present
themselves in the most favorable light possible. If
you speak the language well you will be admired and
promoted." (It was true then, but even truer today.)

"You're a real stickler," Nibs said.

"I don't think so. I don't mean people should speak
pedantically, or sound like an Oxford don, but leaders
seek presentable people who are articulate. Repeating
the same clichés over and over make a person appear
commonplace. Avoid them, avoid platitudes, repetitions
and stutters; and, to repeat, don't even start until you're
sure you're being heard. I say to others: 'Don't rush
things, but remember that on television there's no room
for pauses through which you can drive a truck . Think
like an actor. Just as the actor is judged you will always
be judged based on the way you present yourself.'"

Today's young people, anxious to impress their learned superiors, and rise more quickly in the world, would be well-advised to modify saying "I was like" instead of saying "I said," or "She went" or "He went" instead of "She said," or "He said." I realize slang has its place, but it does not make you more employable.

Nibs was well-spoken and needed no lessons from me in that regard, but, today, the teaching of the proper pronunciation of the English language is deemphasized or completely overlooked in our schools. Our melting pot society, rightly imbued with notions of egalitarianism, allows, and often encourages, the right of its citizens to mangle the language at will.

There are dozens of commonly mispronounced words that show a person to disadvantage. Some, like "temperature" are mispronounced so often they have become the norm even with weather analysts. But if you say the word fast and articulate the " per–a " quickly, you will be saying the word precisely.

Your speech should never sound stiff. But similar to memorizing words or a piece of music, you must, at first, go slowly in your practicing the corrective sounds. Inevitably, the stiffness will fade and your proper articulation will sound natural to you and to others. The process will require you to move your mouth, drop your jaw, and manipulate your tongue and lips, as discussed in Chapter 5.

This is where the effectiveness of the tongue rubdown, mentioned at the end of Chapter 2, has relevance. Here are some words that are commonly mispronounced. Properly employ them if you wish to stand out from the crowd.

| | | |
|---|---|---|
| *pitcher* | *for* | *picture* |
| *perduced* | *for* | *produced* |
| *libarry* | *for* | *library* |
| *diffurnt* | *for* | *different* |
| *calvary* | *for* | *cavalry* |
| *were* | *for* | *we're (pronounced phonetically as "weer")* |
| *ahm* | *for* | *I'm (pronounced "eyem")* |
| *shunt* | *for* | *shouldn't* |
| *dint* | *for* | *didn't (also mispronounced as "did-dint"; it's an elision!)* |
| *perscription* | *for* | *prescription* |
| *perserving* | *for* | *preserving* |
| *probly* | *for* | *probably* |
| *illegedly* | *for* | *allegedly* |
| *reckanize* | *for* | *recognize* |
| *sunn* | *for* | *sudden* |
| *pervent* | *for* | *prevent* |
| *aks* | *for* | *ask* |
| *percedure* | *for* | *procedure* |
| *pertect* | *for* | *protect* |
| *perfessional* | *for* | *professional* |
| *acter* | *for* | *actor* |
| *perducer* | *for* | *producer* |
| *pertection* | *for* | *protection* |
| *curdentials* | *for* | *credentials* |
| *percisely* | *for* | *precisely* |
| *percise* | *for* | *precise* |
| *innerduce* | *for* | *introduce* |
| *plenny* | *for* | *plenty* |
| *inaugarate* | *for* | *inaugurate* |
| *perposed* | *for* | *proposed* |
| *plenny* | *for* | *plenty* |
| *twenny* | *for* | *twenty* |
| *a hunnert* | *for* | *one hundred* |
| *innernational* | *for* | *international* |

I repeat, because it is important: remember, AAAhhm for "I'm" is pronounced and sung EYEM. In order to pronounce it properly, drop your jaw. "We're" is NOT pronounced "were, " as a cowpoke would say, it's pronounced, and sung, and properly enunciated as WEER; " WEER HEER for NEER BEER." ("We're here for near-beer.")

You must pull back your lips and facial muscles. Do not be afraid to, initially, exaggerate. With practice, you will, later, be able to produce these sounds unaffectedly.

"Don't start sentences you can't finish," I continued, speaking with Nibs at our lunch date.

" Don't start sentences and then add other sub-phrases so that I can't follow your train of thought. Compose your sentences. Don't start one and take a wrong turn. Don't wander. Learn to ORGANIZE your thoughts and goals within any presentation of material or presentation of yourself, at a party or anywhere else. Organize as an actor organizes. Everything has a beginning, middle and end. I realize the world is going to pot, but, to quote H.L. Mencken who quotes an Eighteenth century schoolmaster: 'A preposition is a terrible thing to end a sentence with.' Don't end sentences in such manner if you can help it, and if you love the language.

Never allow the last words in any sentence to trail, or drop, off. The last words are sometimes the 'payoff' words in a sentence. Don't swallow them. You may use a downward inflexion, if you like, in reading a sentence, usually for effect, but never allow the cadence of the inflexion to drop so low the final word(s) can't be heard. Choosing higher inflexions, with endings that don't become inaudible, is better. Think of and/or listen to Rex Harrison. Eliminate meaningless pauses. If there's no good reason to move, stand still. Learn to use microphones.

Etiquette is one thing; taste is another. Don't drink out of a bottle. Ask for a glass, or learn to salivate on cue, as actors (and dogs) do. Proper presentation of oneself is largely common sense. 'Clothes are the windows of the Soul,' said Oscar Wilde. Dress for the occasion. You don't wear floppies and shorts to a Shakespeare audition. A man who wears a tie in New York City is treated differently than a man who's tieless.

Sometimes, your reaction to audience stimuli is often more important than the martial which you are delivering. Acting is reacting. Story-board everything like Hitchcock, but be ready to improvise like Fellini.

Just as an actor is taught that the essential thing with dialogue is to find back of the words the experience and behavior that will give them life, the public speaker cannot give an intelligent, caring speech lifelessly and succeed with it."

Our lesson concluded, I was escorting her to the door when Nibs suddenly turned to me and asked why President Reagan had never become a member of the Club.

"Grover Cleveland was a member, why not President Reagan," she whined. I had not lied to her so far, so I told her the truth.

I motioned to her to sit down with me beneath John Singer Sargent's portrait of Joseph Jefferson and related the story of Ronald Reagan and the Players.

"One hundred years after it's founding, Ronald Reagan was about to be nominated for honorary lifetime membership by José Ferrer, who was President of The Club then."

I did not have to tell her who Ferrer was. His portrait as CYRANO de BERGERAC, a role for which he won an Academy Award as Best Actor, was also on the wall and I gestured to it.

"Jo thought Reagan should be made an honorary member," I told her.

"What happened?" Nibs asked in wonder.

"Since one 'No' vote keeps a nominee from being elected to membership, and, since all professional actors are members of at least two unions and, for the most part vote Democratic, Jo was told to reconsider and wisely withdrew Reagan's name," I informed her

"That's terrible!" Nibs squealed. "Terrible!"

"Hey," I said, "Ya wanna be an Actor ya gotta think like an Actor." I had had too much wine at lunch and an aperitif, thereafter, and was, slightly, slurring my words. "It's hard not to empathize with them," I said.

"Empathize?" Nibs echoed, sarcastically.

"It would have been embarrassing if the fortieth President would have lost that particular election, had it been held," I said.

"Huhh!" Nibs replied in an anguished exhalation.

"I'll give it to you a little 'acting for non-actors,' I said. "Here's the way an older actor, especially one who made movies before 1955, would have felt: Ronald Reagan made fifty-six movies, was head of the Screen Actors Guild and a staunch Democrat. Then, according to his son, Ron, Ronald Reagan was appalled when members of the Writers' Guild openly pledged allegiance to the Constitution of the USSR in preference to our own. Supposedly, that was the reason for his

reversal of political sentiments. If true, the reversal
would be understandable. But the former President
of SAG became a Republican and testified before the
House Un-American Activities Committee. He flopped
as a villain in THE KILLERS, Hollywood didn't want
him anymore, and he went to work as a television
spokesman for General Electric. Everyone knows the
story after that."

"Tell me," Nibs said, suddenly a bit belligerently.
I knew I was treading on dangerous terrain but I
continued.

"By that time he had sold his compatriots down
the river, conceding, to the Hollywood studios, actors'
residuals for films made prior to 1955. Out of work, but
appreciated by some, on the Right, for his fronting for
GE on TV, he honed a speaking tour speech extolling
American virtues and the threat of Communism. Right
wing leaders picked up on it and he was picked to make
his famous 'Time for Choosing,' speech for Goldwater.
Because of it he became an underdog candidate in the
Republican primary, eventually becoming Governor of
California.

The issue with older actors is that he sold them
down the river on those residuals. How would you feel?"
I asked her.

"How do YOU feel?" Nibs said, looking deep into
my eyes.

"I think he was a very amiable man. Amiability
is very important,. Making a play or a movie is a
cooperative effort involving many people. There's
a special interaction between the actors. They must
cooperate, even if they're playing roles in which they're
pitted against each other. Developing a reputation for

unfriendliness or haughtiness does not sit well with
others, even though there have been temperamental
stars. NOT getting along brands one as a pariah.
Reagan's M.O. was amiability. According to my friends,
it was genuine. It would be foolish to think otherwise,
and an historical error. "
     That wasn't good enough for her.
     "But what do you really feel? How would YOU have
voted?"
     "Look, I don't agree with any but a couple of his
policies. I think he set the country on the wrong course,
elevating the wealthy and vitiating the policies of FDR.
He accelerated a stupid War on Drugs gave money to
the Contras, threw mental patients on the street, set
back federal housing, wrecked campaign financing ,
helped destroy unions, and cut  social programs while
decreasing taxes on the rich."
     I knew I had gone too far. Nibs looked grim. There
was a long pause before she said,
     "So, what did he do that was so good?"
     "He brought back brown suits."
     She did not laugh, but smiled weakly.
     "Look, I don't follow a Party line; I make my mind
up for myself. He rallied Americans and made most of
them feel good again and he  avoided Nuclear War and,
yes, he did all this because he was sincerely charming.
Listen to his taped phone conversations with Thatcher
and others; hear how he charmed people. That's because
not only was he a good actor, he had something they
don't mention in acting books – WARMTH. That's how
he was able to sustain a relationship with Congress, how
he answered every letter he received, personally"

But this was not enough to mollify her. She was silent as I walked her back to lower Park Avenue and flagged her a cab. Because of the one-sided conversation about her favorite President we did not part on the best of terms and I did not  see or hear from her for some time.

Me and my big mouth!

# 4

# RELAXATION

## *"Take it easy."*
## – BROWNE, MCCLINTON & FREY

I missed seeing or hearing from Nibs.

Had I seen her I would have told her that all the concentration and preparation in the world is for naught without the ability to relax.

The well-rehearsed presentation of self or material fails when fear gains control. Nerves show up in trembling hands, or voice, or in breathlessness, or lack of wind. It's easy to forget what has been rehearsed, and one ends up a fool.

I have rarely heard of an actor who is not nervous before premiering a role on stage and, generally, before every subsequent performance. Many actors, good ones like George C. Scott, vomit on every opening night, as he confessed once on the JOHNNY CARSON Show. Good actors work through their nerves, and become the character they are playing, thus entering another state of mind.

In such cases, nervousness is employed to good effect. When properly harnessed, pent-up energy may evince sincerity and an earnest state of mind. Taken to the extreme, comic geniuses, such as Robin Williams and Richard Pryor, have employed frenetic wit to great effect. If you are in that category, more power to you.

Bing Crosby's casual delivery made him the King of Nonchalance. Those who backed him in sessions

said he seldom took his eyes off the DAILY RACING
FORM, and, then, only to consult a lyric. In fact, Der
Bingle, the most recorded person of all time, was both
well-rehearsed and a practiced improviser, a master of
jazz singing.

The seemingly easygoing Frank Sinatra's well-
deserved reputation as a one-take, no-nonsense film
actor is due to preparedness. Not only did Ole' Blue
Eye hate standing around sweating as lights and camera
placement were being effected, he hated blowing his
lines before cast and crew.

The only person with whom I acted who was
never nervous was Bob Crane, star of the long-running
TV sitcom, HOGAN'S HEROES. I played the role
of his best pal in WHO WAS THAT LADY I SAW
YOU WITH? Funny but unsociable, Crane read the
WALL STREET JOURNAL throughout rehearsals
and between acts, never cracked a smile, never showed
nervousness of any kind, always got his laughs, and
was murdered shortly after the six-week engagement.
His killer, still, at large, allegedly was associated with
Crane's secret "swinger" sex life.

Most actors and performers, and ordinary people
such as you and I, unlike Williams and Pryor, must
analyze, study, prepare, rehearse, and, then, perform
without allowing nervousness to obstruct us from our
goal. There is no secret to relaxation. It is good to loosen
the limbs, crack and manipulate the jaw, massage the
tongue (if no one's looking) and perform knee-bends
and sit-ups. Or go to yoga classes (there are four kinds,
I'm told) take warm baths, and practice meditation one
half-hour daily.

But none of these help much on the spot (except the jaw and tongue bit). The key to relaxation, the only one I know of and which can be called on immediately, is proper breathing. All singers, actors and dancers know that.

I hear you saying, "Getouttathere, I already know how to breathe!" But do you?

If you have never taken acting, singing or dancing classes there is a good chance you have not learned that proper breathing means expansion of the diaphragm, not an expansion and upheaval of the chest. Proper breathing promotes relaxation, concentrates the mind, and calms the nerves.

It seems to me that the forty year-old science of Mindfulness, as reported on and popularized by Anderson Cooper and CBS's 60 MINUTES (12/14/14), is based on the same techniques and principles taught in acting classes. There is no doubt that a calm mind promotes creativity and enhances success in all endeavors. Readers should note that a proper state of Mindfulness is based on, indeed, dependent on proper breathing.

Ironically, on the same evening as the above-mentioned 60 MINUTES airing, CBS's Long Island correspondent, Jennifer McLogan, on affiliate WLNI, reported on the country's first high school to institute a professional, state-of-the-art video facility. It has been in existence for sixty years, and the premise of Logan's reporting was that learning the principles of acting and of on-camera communication promotes "calm" and both mental physical relaxation, the residue of which is a state of confidence. You can't learn to swim sitting by the pool.

When you're nervous – stop! Think and observe
yourself ask, "Am I relaxed?" and if you are not you had
better **start breathing properly**. Never begin a task, a
speech, a meeting, a date, or a political debate without
first breathing deeply and properly. AND STAND UP
STRAIGHT, no slumped shoulders, please!

If you are seated, and you are terribly nervous, clasp
your hands. Sit up straight. Never rotate slightly if the
chair permits such movement. Sit still. Take a pen or
pencil in your hand if you must.

If you are in a televised debate try NOT out-
screaming your opponent. The great American actor-
manger, William Gillette, employed that technique
when introducing SHERLOCK HOLMES to American
audiences, on Broadway, in the year 1900. Gillette, who
also directed the production, staged the affair so that the
entire cast spoke in tones much louder than he, and ran
around the stage in a frenzy, as he proceeded throughout
the play with calm composure.

Relaxation, like everything else in acting, takes
discipline and devotion. Reliant at all times on
consistent proper breathing, the technique must stand
the test in all situations and develop into a skill one can
evoke at will in every situation.

* * * *

Out of the blue one day, a year after our luncheon at
The Players, I received an invitation to Nibs's wedding.
I was very flattered and looked forward to seeing her.
Her note said she profited from our talks and was sorry
we had had a political difference of opinion.

She was a beautiful bride. Nibs married a young doctor from Johns Hopkins who helped found the New York branch of Doctors Without Borders. His name is Tom.

Nibs' parents, it turned out when I met them, were conservative, with a capital "C." But they were friendly people, ranchers, like Reagan. Tom's parents were similarly amiable, but from certain things they said, they were, and remain in their old age, registered Democrats. That was years ago.

Today, Nibs is the CEO of a tech firm in Soho. She is widely known for her communication skills. Her husband has a Park Avenue practice and a free clinic, just off the Bowery. When Tom is away, fighting Ebola, or whatever, Nibs and I go to the theatre. Sometimes we take her teenagers, a boy and a girl, both of whom are preparing to audition for the Juilliard School of Performing Arts.

Nibs and I argue constantly about Reagan and politics, generally, but we both agree that what Ronald Reagan learned as an actor placed him in a position from which he changed the course of the country and the world.

If Nibs and I can get along I do not see why the country cannot do the same.

# 5

# ARTICULATION
## THE VOICE AND PROPER PRONUNCIATION OF THE ENGLISH LANGUAGE

*"Speech is the mirror of the soul."*
- PUBLILIUS SYRUS C. 50 B.C.

*"Speak the speech, I pray you, as I pronounced*
*it to you, trippingly, on the tongue."*
- WILLIAM SHAKESPEARE

Nibs speaks beautifully. Hers is not a back-of-the-throat, gurgled little-girl voice. Her sound is produced from her mask, not from down-deep in her esophagus. She has learned the meaning of placement.

Her voice is resonant and well-modulated, and she has that quality endemic to good acting – a sense of rhythm and tone. She has taken singing lessons. She knows the head-buzz achieved from proper placement. Her breathing is similarly appropriate and she produces a sufficient passage of air across the vocal chords to create a pleasant sound. She knows to drop her jaw and, thus, avoid nasality. Nibs does not produce this sound consciously anymore and has no need of practice. She never sounds affected.

I did give her an exercise which, aside from massaging the tongue, she uses to this day when she wants to sound A-Okay. She sings a scale, consisting of seven childish notes. You may adapt it to whichever key is comfortable. I give it to you in the key of C, thusly: C – G - E - C, going up the scale, and E – G – C, going down. Employ, initially, the sound of "Ah" what we call the "broad A" in mid-Atlantic speech, the proper enunciation of English as taught to American actors for decades. Switch to an "o" sound, then "ee" and similarly, the other vowel sounds listed below.

Then, using the "mmmm" sound only, hum for long notes and, finally, execute the same scale singing-humming "mmmm." Resonance should result. Hold your fingertips to your temple. A buzz vibrates from there to the top of your head.

The main objective of the mid-Atlantic speech sound is the elimination, in one's speech, of Gladdic Shock which occurs in a too sharply-spoken "a's" and "ah's." Gladdic shock is most evident in the speech of my fellow Midwesterners and the ugly, explosive sound they deliver on words such as "after" and "action."

Again, language is the medium within which we operate. Do not be stereotyped. With will power and practice ANYONE MAY LEARN TO SPEAK "PERFECT" ENGLISH, no matter their ethnic background.

If you refuse to allocate practice-time, in order to reach your goal, if you, simply, rely on improving though listening to others, it will require years. But if you practice enough you will speak "the King's English."

My Father spoke without an accent of any kind. Born in Russia, he spoke only that tongue until his arrival in America. My son's college instructor in English, a man considerably younger than I, insists there is no such thing as "good" or "bad" English; everything is permissible; anything goes and that includes "Ebonics" (a word attributed to Robin Williams).

It is, for instance, okay with my son's English professor, to say "ax" instead of "ask." I agree that English derives from numerous sources, Anglo-Saxon, Arabic, French, Spanish, Native American, Yiddish and African-American among them. I enjoy and employ slang and am a student of H.L. Mencken's AMERICAN LANGUAGE in all its editions and supplements.

I have had, in my classes and privately, African-American students (some from Africa, too) who, having had little experience of pronouncing, or hearing "ask" pronounced properly, now, wanted to learn to say it precisely and with ease. It is, simply, a matter of the proper formation of the mouth and jaw and manipulation of the tongue (whether placed at the roof of the mouth or the back of the teeth) and lips.

To say "ask" properly: say "ass" first. Drop your jaw in an exaggerated manner in approaching the "aah" sound. Repeat it a few times. Then, continuing to drop the jaw exaggeratedly on the "ahh" add "kuh" to it. Say "ass" and end it with "kuh." After awhile, drop the "kuh" and keep the "k" It is now "ass" with "k" on the end, as it should be.

I realize we are living at a time when swinishness is celebrated and that the language of Donne, Shakespeare, Churchill, Lincoln, Frederick Douglass and Martin Luther King is in the process of daily desecration, but the elision of, and/or disregard for the necessary dotting of, the letter "t" amounts to a national disgrace.

Not universally, but with frequency, "fi – ing" has replaced "fighting." "Light" has become "lii – uh." Mountains have become "Moun – uns."The letter "t" is missing altogether, and crossing the "t" seems too difficult for the modern man or woman to enunciate.

The fact is "t" is, again, a simple matter of placing the
tip of the tongue at the roof of the mouth, just behind the
upper teeth. Simple words, such as "matter," "button,"
the aforementioned "plenty," "twenty," and others of
that ilk, fit the category of the mispronounced "t.'s."

To these add "Manhattan" and "Staten Island,"
which, now desecrated, have become "Man – ha –un."
and "Stat – un" Island, respectively. The "t" should
properly be preceded by a complete dropping of the jaw
on the "a" in "Man" and the "ha" in "hat."

It is likewise unnerving that "didn't" is turning
into "di – un,"or "did – dint," or, just plain old, "dint."
Enunciating the word properly requires sounding the
second "d" just as the first, i.e., by spreading the lips in
a smile and placing the tongue at the back of the lower
teeth: "did – int." Of course, the "t" must be crossed at
the end of the word. Webster's Dictionary lists the word
phonetically, as it is written: "didn't."

You can improve your speech by mastering the
sounds in this chapter. Learn to form the sounds with
your mouth by properly positioning your tongue and
lips, breathing properly and passing air across the palate
while dropping the jaw when necessary. Repeat them
over and over until they sound natural. Recording and
listening to playbacks will speed your progress.

If you feel silly and affected hearing these sounds
played back, that's your problem. You must overcome
such a silly thing as feeling silly about improving the
quality of your voice. If you haven't the time to devote,
that is another matter and the result will be that you
(and others) will have to listen to the ugly sound of
your voice for the rest of your life. Your goal is to speak
properly and without affectation.

The following is a list of the sounds of the vowels
and consonants in our language. In order to speak
properly they must be mastered. Get a tape recorder;
speak them into the microphone. See if you are happy
with the way you sound. Practice for improvement.

# VOWELS

Remember to drop your jaw on the broad sounds
and manipulate the jaw and lips properly for the others
when saying the following. Exaggerate and draw out  the
sounds until you get them right.

| AH | O | AWE | OH | OO |
|---|---|---|---|---|
| past | rod | taught | loud | coot |
| father | rot | horse | crowd | hoot |
| path | pod | bought | know | boot |
| bath | sod | ought | coal | boom |
| half | cod | forced | rose | food |
| laugh | body | halt | though | cool |
| calf | shot | all | nose | soothe |
| ask | knock | call | own | roof |
| past | clock | haul | folk | spouse |
| straw | moth | warm | close | smooth |
| dance | Todd | dorm | hole | move |
| pass | golf | ball | boat | tooth |
| darn | cough | moth | open | school |
| craft | lost | launch | road | choose |

| Ah | Uh | Er | A | Eh |
|---|---|---|---|---|
| blast | thus | purse | thanks | egg |
| chance | tub | surreal | prance | felt |
| chant | come | nurse | can | bread |
| slant | flush | firm | that | let |
| rather | sun | learn | gas | friend |

| psalm | shut | squirm | patch | twelve |
|-------|------|--------|-------|--------|
| bright | club | thirsty | fancy | American |
| glance | truck | murky | gather | man |

OO        OH        AWE        O        AH

Here's how to think of these early vowels. Start with lips drawn close together in the "OO." Then, go through all of the positions in a slow manner, (don't rush), until you come to "Ah." Make sure each sound is different, one from the other. Take breaths in between sounds. Each must be distinctly different. Let one sound come to an end before going to the succeeding one. Still, let the lips relax back to the normal position only after "Ah" is finished sounding, so that there is no moving of the lips except to open between every sound.

In both the foregoing and in the following vowel sounds, remember that the process is one of passing breath across the vocal chords. For purposes of these exercises emphasize this procedure, then, bring it back to normal. Observe the introduction of compound vowels and dipthongs, where one vowel sound leads to another.

| Aye | I | Ee | Ah-I | I-er |
|-----|---|-----|------|------|
| bay | wish | beef | night | year |
| they | stiff | dream | bright | sneer |
| faint | thick | me | cry | mere |
| whale | limp | speak | flier | queer |
| frame | scrimp | tea | sigh | rear |
| fame | shrimp | speak | fight | dear |
| blame | film | leap | flight | hear |
| play | kiln | pea | kite | fear |
| whale | victim | sleep | height | seer |
| say | milk | street | ice | tea |

| Eh-er | I-Oo | Ah-Oo | Awe-I |
|-------|------|-------|-------|
| prayer | duke *not dook* | pound | noise |
| square | knew *not knoo* | how | oil |
| rare | stew *not stoo* | brow | annoy |
| fair | Yule *not Yool* | allow | foil |
| tear | sewer *not sooer* | drown | voice |
| swear | sue *not soo* | thou | employ |
| chair | lure *not loor* | thousand | soil |
| mare | nude *not nood* | noun | noise |
| vary | resume *not resoom* | cloud | boy |

Remember, any list of words is inadequate. It might be an edifying experience for the reader to add similar words of your own choosing to the above lists. Here are lists comprised of front, mid and back vowels, along with diphthongs, all worthy of practice:

| Front | Mid | Back | Diphthongs |
|-------|-----|------|------------|
| we | up | chorus | may |
| will | further | too | joe |
| fast | | all | you |
| mad | | books | I |
| them | | lid | join |
| make | | wants | now |

Now, make sentences out of the last two columns and repeat them slowly.

Another vocal exercise involving vowels:

| | |
|------|------|
| BOY | PONY |
| DOG | TOY |
| GEEK | KEY |
| GUN | OUT |

And another good list for practice; move your mouth and lips:

| | |
|---|---|
| RUBBER | WRING |
| RAFTER | WIRING |
| RASTRA | WORE |
| RAFT | WRECKAGE |
| ROLLING | WRECK |
| RALPH | WREN |
| ROCK | WRESTLING |
| RUSHING | WRESTLE |
| ROLL | WREATH |
| ROULETTE | WRATH |
| ROLLIFLEX | WORLD |
| ROBIN | WHIRLED |
| RAP | WRAP |

# CONSONANTS

1. ASPIRANTS – which are soundless, i.e., a.) unimpeded H and b.) impeded F.

2. VIBRANTS - M, N and V

3. EXPLOSIVES – P, T and K

4. SOUNDING EXPLOSIVES – B and D, which vibrate.

5. SIBBILANTS - S

6. UNCLASSIFIED - L and R

Bite off the explosives. Use the lips and the tip of the tongue. I recommend listening to recorded plays, old radio shows, and Shakespeare. Improving one's speech is a matter of diligence but the payoff is considerable.

1.  EXPLOSIVES – Especially those involving t's and d's: Place tongue at roof of mouth just back of your top teeth in order to cross t's and properly say: Chatter, Chapter, Matter

Likewise, try to say students (crossing the "t") instead of "student Practice double "t" words.

I know of no word "impordant," it's IMPORTANT, i.e., place the tongue behind top teeth. Say "tuh" and gradually, make the "t" explode  comfortably behind the teeth. It's not necessary to sound Shakespearean, but it's "victim" not "victum;" "excited' not "etcited," and in the Arctic it is pronounced "ARK – TIK" not "ar-tic."

But don't feel badly; these are common mistakes and I composed this list, largely, from newscasters mistakes, folks who are, supposedly, paid to pronounce words properly. By the way, if you're feeling that if you learn to speak too well you may lose your illiterate friends, think of it this way – actors play many roles and it is entirely permissible for you to act one way with your friends and an entirely different way when you check into The Breakers in Miami Beach or approach the president of your bank for a loan.  Actors are taught to be many things to many people.

At the end of the day (one of my least favorite of current cliches), it is well to remember that acting, whether it is a craft or an art, requires a wealth of qualities, the possession of any of which would be a blessing to the non-actor. Among them, and those elucidated above, are imagination, the power to visualize and recreate, sharpened sensibilities, acuteness of perception, human warmth, personality, magnetism, mimetic sense, dramatic sense, recognition of conflict, a sense of style, and, above all, something we all dearly need in these trying times, courage.

# INDEX

# ABOUT THE AUTHOR

Sidney Eden has acted with, directed and, as a producer, presented many of the biggest stars of stage and screen. Mentored by Jose Ferrer, Jose Quintero, John Cassavttes and Milton Katselas, Eden created ACTING FOR NON-ACTORS, in New York City, in the early 1980's. Tailored to meet the needs of non-actors in diverse fields, from doctors and lawyers to cab drivers and cops, the course has attracted thousands. Beginning his professional career as a teenaged actor at the renowned Cleveland Playhouse, Eden has played with and/or opposite Martha Raye, Kay Ballard, Bob Crane, Craig Stevens, Barnard Hughes, Hugh O'Brian, Ed Binns, Peter Breck, Constance Towers, Dom De Luise, June Squibb and others, in stock and on and off-Broadway, in a wide range of plays, from ARE YOU NOW OR HAVE YOU EVER BEEN, starring Liza Minnelli, Tammy Grimes and Dina Merrill, to Julian (LENNY) Barry's controversial SITCOM, at the fabled St. Nicholas Theatre Company, founded by David Mamet and W.H. "Bill" Macy (of SHAMELESS fame), in which Eden created the leading role of Leonard Poetry. He has appeared in numerous commercials, on and off-camera, on all the major soaps, and in the movies CHAPTER TWO, CONFLICT OF INTEREST, and the celebrated guerilla film, SPOOK WHO SAT BY THE DOOR, directed by Ivan Dixon. Eden has directed dozens of plays

and musicals, including GUYS & DOLLS, with Alan
Alda, Edgar Bergen, in YOU CAN'T TAKE IT WITH
YOU, and Larry Parks and Betty Garrett, in HIGH
BUTTON SHOES, at prestigious theatres, such as the
Goodman Theatre of the Art Institute of Chicago, the
Brooklyn Academy of Music, the Cleveland Playhouse
and the State Theatre of Maine. Eden produced and
directed a national summer tour of A RAISIN IN THE
SUN, starring Claudia McNeil, and a group of, then,
unknowns – Gail Fisher, Al Freeman, Jr., Raymond
St. Jacques and Gloria Foster. Just prior, he served as
Production Supervisor for Oscar Brown, Jr.'s legendary
KICKS & Co., starring Burgess Meredith and Nichelle
Nichols, directed by the iconic playwright, Lorraine
Hansberry. Eden founded the First Chicago Center,
the first first-class theater in the Loop in decades,
creating an international hit with his revival of Eugene
O'Neill's HUGHIE, starring Ben Gazzara (Tony-
nominated). He, then, presented and launched a national
tour of his prize-winning production of WHEN YOU
COMIN' BACK, RED RYDER? starring playwright
Mark Medoff. Eden's GEORGE JEAN NATHAN IN
REVUE, a play of his own authorship based on the
works of the famous theatre critic, was successfully
produced at Goodman, his MENCKEN, NATHAN
& GOD, at the Lincoln Center Workshop, and his
ATLANTIC CITY LOST, off-Broadway. TV critic for
NBC-TEMPO, on the nationally televised BROADWAY
MAGAZINE, Eden is, also, a singer-pianist who has
recorded with jazz greats Joe Albany (subject of the film
LOWDOWN), Zoot Sims, Clark Terry, Mel Lewis and
others. Eden has written on numerous occasions for the
VILLAGE VOICE.

Website: sideden.com
E-mail: acting4nonactors@gmail.com

ACKNOWWLEDGEMENTS:
Ms. Denise Garrett and Ms. Ingrid Abbott of the
United States Library of Congress TX Division

# NOTES

CPSIA information can be obtained
at www.ICGtesting.com
Printed in the USA
FFOW02n1447261015
17966FF